A NEW INTRODUCTION

Stories of Jesus and His Teaching

R H HORTON · REDVERS BRANDLING

Illustrated by Juliette Palmer

Hodder & Stoughton

LONDON SYDNEY AUCKLAND TORONTO

British Library Cataloguing in Publication Data

© 1962 Robert H Horton
© 1990 Robert H Horton and Redvers Brandling

ISBN 0 340 52354 9

First published 1962
Second Edition 1990

All rights reserved. No part of this publication may be
reproduced or transmitted in any form or by any means,
electronic or mechanical, including photocopy, recording,
or any information storage and retrieval system, without
permission in writing from the publisher or under licence
from the Copyright Licensing Agency Limited. Further
details of such licences (for reprographic reproduction) may
be obtained from the Copyright Licensing Agency Limited,
of 33–34 Alfred Place, London WC1E 7DP.

Typeset by Taurus Graphics, Abingdon.
Printed in Great Britain for the educational publishing
division of Hodder and Stoughton Ltd, Mill Road, Dunton
Green, Sevenoaks, Kent by Richard Clay Ltd, Bungay.

Preface

This series, *A New Introduction to the Bible*, is made up of four books and four accompanying blackline master workpacks. It has been written for the 9–13 age range and forms a complete Religious Education resource at this level.

The stories in the four books have been taken from Robert Horton's series *An Introduction to the Bible*. These stories have not been altered in any way because they still 'satisfy a pressing need for a simple and straightforward account of the Bible story, told in a language which can be readily understood'.

New question sections have been written by Redvers Brandling and these are set at the end of each story and labelled 'Over to you'. They have been carefully written with modern thinking about assessment and assessment techniques clearly in mind so that they not only test knowledge and comprehension, but also fit into the wider context of whole curriculum planning.

The workpacks which accompany the four books, one pack per book, further support the work begun in the 'Over to you' sections. There is one worksheet per story and the work set here is widely varied in order to develop as many skills as possible. The range of tasks includes Cloze procedure, crosswords, wordsearches, all forms of creative and formal writing exercises, and visual/artwork exercises such as enlarging pictures and illustrating text.

The books and packs have been carefully designed for ease of use and are fully illustrated throughout. In the case of the books the ever-popular illustrations drawn for Horton's series have been retained because of their suitability as artwork resource material. As a series *A New Introduction to the Bible* forms a complete course of work which is appropriate for use with pupils of all abilities and from all religious backgrounds.

Contents

The Birth of Jesus

On the edge of the Roman Empire was the small country of
Palestine. In the little town of Nazareth, in the north of
Palestine, lived a girl named Mary. She was to marry a
carpenter named Joseph. One day, God sent his angel to Mary,
and he told her, 'You shall have a son, and you shall name him
Jesus.' The boy was to be Mary's baby, but he was also to be
God's Son.

Before the baby was born, Mary and Joseph had to go to
Bethlehem, in the south of the country. At that time the
Romans ruled Palestine, and the Roman Emperor had made an
order that all the people must be counted so that they could be
taxed. Now Joseph was of the family of the great king David,
whose city was Bethlehem. So it was to Bethlehem that Joseph
had to go.

THE GREAT SEA

CAESAREA PHILIPPI

CAPERNAUM

MAGDALA · SEA OF GALILEE

CANA

NAZARETH

NAIN

GALILEE

SAMARIA

SAMARIA

RIVER JORDAN

PALESTINE
IN THE TIME
OF JESUS

EMMAUS

JERUSALEM

BETHLEHEM

BETHANY

JERICHO

JUDEA

DEAD SEA

EGYPT

MILES

0 20 30 40 50

Slowly, Mary and Joseph made their way to the south. Mary rode on an ass, while Joseph walked along beside her. When, at last, they came to Bethlehem they found that the inn was full. There was no place where they could stay. But at last the

The shepherds found Jesus lying in a manger.

innkeeper found them a stable. It was not a very fine place, but at least it was warm and dry. In this stable, during the night, the baby Jesus was born, and Mary laid him in a manger to sleep. The manger was a trough made of wood which held the hay for the animals to eat. It made a good bed for the little child.

Outside Bethlehem, on the hillside, something wonderful was happening. Some shepherds were there, looking after their sheep in the darkness. Suddenly, they saw a great light, and the angel of God came to them. The shepherds were very much afraid, and hid their eyes from the great light. Then the angel spoke to them.

'Don't be afraid,' he said, 'for I bring you good news.' Then he told them all about the baby Jesus, and where they could go to see him. They heard the song of many angels in the sky, and then all was dark and quiet as before.

The shepherds looked at one another and said, 'Let us go to Bethlehem at once, and see this great sight.' They left their sheep and made their way to the town. There they found Mary and Joseph in the stable, and the baby Jesus lying in the manger, just as the angel had said. Full of joy they went out and told the people all that had happened.

Your turn now . . .

Research and discussion

1 Read verses 3–4 of Luke, Chapter 2.

2 When you have read these discuss the following with your friends and teacher.
   a) Why did Joseph have to go to Bethlehem?
   b) Look at the map. What sort of journey do you think Mary and Joseph faced?
   c) What must have been particularly worrying for both Joseph and Mary?

Writing

Write down the meaning of the following words. Use a dictionary where necessary:
   carpenter   taxed   manger

Drama

With your friends act out two dramas.
a) The first should be from the time Mary and Joseph arrive at the inn, until they are settled in the stable.
b) The second should be the shepherds' experience on the hillside.
As you prepare your dramas use the following words to give you some ideas:
a) worry – disappointment – concern – inadequate – relief – contentment;
b) unease – shock – disbelief – fear – exultation – pride – joy.

2

The Wise Men

One day some wise men came to Jerusalem. They had come from a land in the East, and they were looking for the king of the Jews. These men had seen a great and wonderful new star in the sky, and it was a sign to them that a king had been born. As the royal palace was in Jerusalem they thought that they would find the baby king there. So they came to the palace, and King Herod sent for them.

Herod heard the story told by the wise men, and he wondered who this new King of the Jews could be. He sent for the priests and asked them about their holy books.

'Where does it say that Christ will be born?' Herod asked them. The name Christ is the same name as Messiah and it means the Anointed One, the One sent by God.

The priests told him that Christ was to be born in Bethlehem. So Herod told the wise men that they must go to Bethlehem and look for the baby. When they had found him they were to come back and tell Herod so that he, too, could go and worship him. This was not true, for Herod was afraid of the new king, and he wanted to kill him.

As the wise men left Jerusalem they saw the star again leading them to Bethlehem. In haste, they came to the town and there they saw the great star, still and bright, over the stable where Jesus lay. Quietly they went in and knelt in front of the child. Then they took out the gifts they had brought for him, and laid them before him.

In a dream, they were told by God that they must not go back to Herod, and they went home to their own land by another way. Joseph, too, had a dream. An angel told him that he must take the child and Mary away.

'Take the child and his mother to Egypt,' said the angel, 'for Herod will try to kill him.'

That night, Joseph did as he had been told, and they fled to Egypt. Herod was very angry when the wise men did not come back. He gave orders that all the baby boys in or near Bethlehem, who were under two years old, must be killed. Then there would be no other king but himself. He did not know that Jesus was already far away and safe from him.

At last, Herod died, and it was safe for Joseph to bring Jesus

The wise men saw a great new star in the sky.

and Mary back home. So they came back to their own land, and to their own town of Nazareth.

Your turn now . . .

Research and writing

I When you have read the story carefully answer the following questions in sentences.

   a) What mistake did the wise men make when they arrived from the East?

   b) What did Herod ask them?

   c) How did Herod seek to use the wise men to find out where Jesus was?

   d) Why didn't the wise men return to Jerusalem?

   e) Where was Joseph told to take Mary and Jesus?

   f) What was Herod's plan to make sure Jesus was killed?

g) When was it safe for Mary, Joseph and Jesus to return to their own land?

2 Look at these words: Christ – Messiah – the Anointed One. Write down what they have in common.

Drama

Read Matthew, Chaper 2, verse 11.
Now, with some friends, act out the scene where the wise men deliver their gifts. Make sure you know what the gifts are.

—— 3 ——

The Boyhood of Jesus

In our Bible we can read the stories of Jesus as a baby, the stories we have read in the first two chapters of this book. Then there are many stories about Jesus as a man who began to teach and heal when he was about thirty years old. There is only one story about Jesus as a boy.

This story is about a special feast, the Feast of the Passover. This was a very important time, when all the Jews remembered the coming of Egypt many years before. All good Jews tried to go to the great Temple at Jerusalem for this feast. The Temple was the House of God.

Each year, Mary and Joseph went to Jerusalem at Passover time. When Jesus was twelve years old they took him with them. What a great day it was for Jesus, as it was for every Jewish boy, when he went to the Temple in the great city.

At the end of the Feast, Mary and Joseph set off for home again. Jesus was not with them, but they thought that he was with their friends and relations. But, as the day went on, they began to look for him. He was nowhere to be found: Jesus had stayed behind in Jerusalem.

There was only one thing to be done. Mary and Joseph turned back and hurried to the city gates. They were very anxious. For three long days they looked for Jesus, and then, at last, they found him. He was in the Court of the Temple, sitting among

Jesus was in the Temple, sitting among the teachers.

the teachers, listening and asking questions. Everyone was amazed at the clever words of this young boy.

How glad Mary was to see Jesus again. She told him how anxious she and Joseph had been. The answer of Jesus showed that, already, he was getting ready to do God's work.

'Why did you look for me?' he asked. 'Didn't you know that I must be doing my Father's work?'

Mary and Joseph did not understand what Jesus meant, but they were glad to take him home with them to Nazareth. Here he settled down with them at home. We think that he must have helped his mother in the house, and his father in the carpenter's shop. So the years passed by, and Jesus grew up.

Research and discussion

Discuss each of the following with your friends and teacher.
a) How Mary and Joseph felt when they discovered Jesus was lost.
b) What they did during the three days it took to find him.
c) What different feelings they must have had when they found him.
d) Why they could not understand about his staying behind.

Writing

Write down the meaning of the following words. Use a dictionary if necessary: temple   relations   anxious.

Talking

Imagine you have been asked to give a talk about the only story of Jesus' boyhood. Prepare it very carefully. Make sure that your facts are right and decide the order in which you are going to tell them. Make your talk last about two minutes.

—— 4 ——

John the Baptist

Just before the birth of Jesus another baby was born. When he grew up he was to play an important part in the life of Jesus, so his story must be told here.

Mary, the mother of Jesus, had a cousin named Elisabeth. Her husband, Zacharias, was a priest in the Temple at Jerusalem. It was the work of the priests to lead the worship of God at the Temple. Elisabeth and Zacharias were getting old and they had no children. One day, as Zacharias stood by the altar in the Temple, an angel spoke to him.

'You shall have a son,' said the angel, 'and you shall call him John.'

'How can I know that this is true?' asked the old priest, for he could not believe it.

The angel told him that, because he doubted, he would be dumb until the child was named.

When the baby was born everyone wanted to call him Zacharias, after his father. But his mother said that he must be called John. Then his father was asked and, not being able to speak, he wrote down the name, John. At once he was able to speak again.

People thought that John would grow up to be a priest like his father. But when he grew up John went away into the desert, to live alone and to think about God. And God had a plan for him. John was to be the one who prepared the people for the coming of God's Son, Jesus the Christ.

From the desert John came down to the river Jordan and there he preached to the people who passed by. Many others heard about him and came to see this strange man from the desert. John told them that they must all live better lives.

'Why, what must we do?' they asked him.

'You must all be kind to one another,' said John. 'You tax-collectors must not take more tax-money than is right. You

Two of the men who went to hear John the Baptist. One is a tax-collector, the other is a leader of the Jewish religion, a Pharisee.

soldiers must not treat people badly.'

All those who wanted to live better lives were baptised in the river by John. Some of them thought that John was the Christ for whom they had waited for so many years. But John told them that he was not the Christ.

'There is One coming who is far greater than I am. I am not fit even to undo his shoes.'

Your turn now...

Research and writing

Write sentences to answer each of the following questions.
a) Was Jesus related to John?
b) What punishment was inflicted on Zacharias and why was this?
c) What did most people expect John to become?
d) Where did John make his home?
e) Why do you think he was called the 'Baptist'?

Discussion

Discuss the following points with your friends and teachers.
a) What sort of physical qualities do you think John needed?
b) How do you think John built up his reputation?
c) Why might people want to live 'better lives'?
d) Did John know he was preparing the way for Jesus?

Reading

By reading Mark, Chapter 1, verse 6 you will find out how John dressed and what he ate in the desert.

—— 5 ——

The Baptism and Temptation of Jesus

One wonderful day, Jesus himself came from Nazareth to the river Jordan where John was baptising the people. When Jesus asked John to baptise him too, John did not want to do it.

'No!' said John. 'It is you who should baptise me.'

But at last John did what Jesus wanted, and together they went down into the water.

As they came out again from the river, a great light shone from the sky. The Spirit of God came down upon Jesus in the shape of a dove, and God's voice was heard:

'This is my beloved Son, in whom I am well pleased.'

After his baptism Jesus went away into the desert, alone. He wanted to think and pray. For forty days and nights he was there without any food. While he was in the desert Jesus was tempted by the devil to use his power in ways that he knew were wrong.

First, the devil tempted Jesus to turn the stones at his feet into bread. Jesus was very hungry, but he would not do this.

John baptised Jesus in the river Jordan.

'Man does not live only by bread,' he said to the devil, 'but by the word of God.'

Next, the devil took Jesus to the top of the great Temple in Jerusalem, where he stood high above the street and the people. He told Jesus to jump down, for the angels would see that he came to no harm. Again Jesus refused to do as the devil asked.

'You must not tempt the Lord your God,' he said.

Then the devil took Jesus to the top of a high mountain and showed him all the lands round about them.

'All these lands can be yours,' said the devil, 'if you will only worship me.'

'Get behind me,' said Jesus, 'for you must worship only God.'

When the three temptations were over the devil left Jesus alone. He was ready now to begin his work of teaching and healing the people, the work that God had sent him to do.

Your turn now...

Research and discussion

Discuss the following points with your friends and teacher.
a) Why didn't John want to baptise Jesus?
b) What feelings might John have had after the ceremony?
c) Why did Jesus go into the desert?

Writing

Read through the chapter again and then write down the exact words spoken by Jesus and the devil during the time of temptation.

Drama

Imagine the scene: John busy at the river, crowds of people mingling round, the sudden arrival of Jesus, John recognises him, Jesus indicates what he wants. What happens next?

Now, with friends, prepare a mime of this scene. Remember no words must be spoken. Try to make your hands, faces and movements show all the emotions necessary.

—— 6 ——

John the Baptist in Prison

In Chapter 4 we read how John the Baptist went into the desert to think about God, and how he came down to the river Jordan to preach and to baptise the people who wanted to live better lives. John was never afraid to say what he thought was right, and this was to get him into trouble with Herod, the king.

This Herod was not, of course, the king who had tried to put the baby Jesus to death. That was Herod the Great, and this king was his son. Herod had married a woman named Herodias, who was already the wife of Philip, a half-brother of Herod. John said that this was not lawful, and so Herod put him in prison. This pleased Herodias, who was very angry at what John had said. She would have liked to see John put to death, but Herod did not want to do this.

While John was in prison he began to wonder about Jesus. Was he really the Christ for whom the Jews had waited for so long? He sent two of his friends to ask Jesus if he were the Christ. Jesus sent the men back to John to tell him about all the wonderful things that he was doing.

'Tell John,' said Jesus, 'how the blind are made to see, the lame can walk, lepers are healed, the deaf can hear, and the dead are brought to life again.'

When John heard this, he knew the answer to his question: Jesus really was the Christ.

Herod put John the Baptist in prison.

On his birthday, King Herod held a feast for all the great people of the land. There were many fine things to eat and to drink. After the meal, the daughter of Herodias, whose name was Salome (Sa-low-mi), came in to dance. She danced so well that Herod made a rash promise that he would give her anything she asked for, up to half of his kingdom.

Salome asked her mother what she should take. Herodias, who hated John for what he had said, saw her chance to get rid of him. She told Salome to ask for John the Baptist's head. The king was sorry when he heard this, but he had made a promise. He did not want to go back on his word in front of all these people. So, at the order of the king, John was put to death in his prison cell, and his head was given to Salome. Later John's friends took away John's body to bury it.

Your turn now . . .

Research and writing

1 Answer the following questions in sentences.
  a) Can you give an example of John's courage?
  b) What did John think about when he was in prison?
  c) Why was John imprisoned
  d) Why was King Herod having a feast?
  e) Who entertained the king and his guests?
  f) What was the promise Herod made?
  g) Why didn't Herod break his promise when he heard Salome's terrible request?

2 Write down the meanings of the following words. Use a dictionary where necessary: lawful   lepers   rash.

3 Imagine you are a radio reporter working for Time and Space broadcasting station. You are sent back in time to Herod's feast to describe the events to your listeners. Think carefully about your description; make notes for it; record your broadcast.
Use the following words to help:

celebration – excitement – dangerous – dread – horror
luxury – entertainment

Two Miracles at Cana

Not far from Nazareth, the home of Jesus, was a town called Cana. The map on page 6 will show you where these two towns were. One day there was a wedding at Cana, and Jesus was there with his mother and his disciples.

As the feast went on it was found that there was no wine left. When Mary heard about this she told Jesus. She did not know what he would do, but she told the servants to do whatever he told them. There were some water-pots in the courtyard of the house, and Jesus told the servants to fill them with water. Then they were to fill the wine-jars from the water-pots and take them into the feast. The servants did as they were told and carried the jars into the feast. Then it was found that they were filled, not with water, but with wine, far better than the wine

Jesus told the servants to fill the wine jars with water.

that had already been drunk. The guests at the wedding were surprised at the taste. It was the custom to serve the best wine first, and then the poor wine later. But at this feast the best wine had been saved to the last. This was Jesus's first miracle.

Some time later, Jesus was in Cana again. A great man, who lived in Capernaum (see map), had heard that Jesus was there, and he had come to ask his help. The man was very worried about his son, who was dying. He asked Jesus if he would come and heal him.

'Go home!' said Jesus. 'Your son is well.'

The man believed what Jesus had said, and gladly set off for his home. On the way some of his servants met him, and told him that his son was well again. The father was full of joy at this wonderful news.

'At what time did he begin to get well?' he asked the servants. When he was told, he knew that it was the exact time when Jesus had told him that his son was well.

Your turn now . . .

Research and discussion

Check the passage for information and then discuss the following questions with your friends and teacher.

a) Why do you think the guests were usually served the best wine first?

b) How did the man from Capernaum show trust?

c) What sort of words do you think the servants might have used when they ran out to meet their master?

Writing

a) Imagine that you were a guest at the wedding at Cana. Later you write a letter to a friend saying what fantastic things happened there. Write this letter.

b) Imagine that you were the man from Capernaum whose son's life was saved. After this you write a letter to Jesus. Write this letter.

Jesus begins to Preach

When Jesus began to preach he left his home town of Nazareth and went to live in Capernaum. This town was on the edge of the Sea of Galilee. It was a better centre for his work as he went about the country.

One Sabbath Jesus went back to Nazareth and went into the synagogue there. The synagogue was the Jewish church where

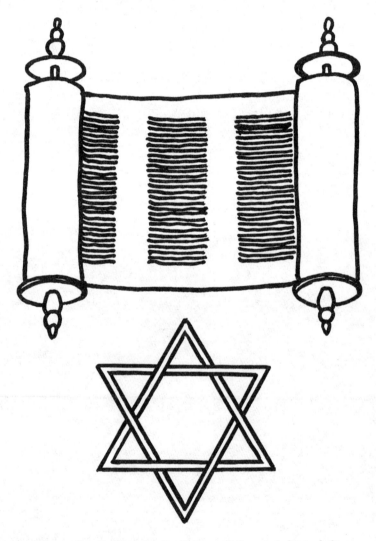

Above: *A scroll or book: it is read from right to left.*
Below: *The Star of David, to be found in every synagogue.*

men went to hear the word of God: women were not allowed in the main part of the synagogue but had to go in a kind of gallery. The ruler of the synagogue at Nazareth asked Jesus to read and to speak to the people. Visiting preachers were often asked to do this. So Jesus took up the book (or scroll) of the prophet Isaiah. There were many books by the prophets who were men sent by God to speak to his people many years ago.

After he had read, Jesus sat down to talk to the people about what Isaiah had said. At first all the men were amazed at how well he spoke. Then they remembered that he was only the son of a local carpenter. How was it that such a man could speak so well? They did not like some of the things that Jesus had to say. He tried to show them that God was not only the God of the Jews but the God of all nations. He told them stories of God's kindness to people who were not Jews in days long ago. Some of the men grew angry.

All at once these got up and rushed Jesus out of their synagogue. They took him to the edge of the hill on which Nazareth was built and were ready to push him over. Somehow not one of them was able to do this. Jesus turned quietly and walked away through the crowd. He was never able to do any great miracle at Nazareth as the people had no faith in him.

So Jesus went back to Capernaum and preached in the synagogue there. One Sabbath there was a sick man in this synagogue and Jesus healed him. Then he went to the house of a man named Simon Peter where he found Peter's mother-in-law very ill with fever. Jesus took her hand and she was well again at once. She began to get a meal ready for Jesus and his disciples as if she had never been ill at all.

As it was the Sabbath when no one must work, the people of the town could not carry their sick ones to Jesus. They had to wait until the sun went down, for at sunset the Sabbath was over. Then many sick people were brought to Jesus, crowding the street outside Peter's house. Jesus went out to them and healed them all.

Your turn now . . .

Research and writing

1 Write your opinions about the following statements.
  a) Jesus thought about a good centre from which he could

work.

b) Anybody might be asked to preach in the synagogue.

c) The son of a carpenter might be expected to be a great scholar.

d) Jesus was very well thought of in Nazareth.

2 Read Luke, Chapter 4, verses 28–30 and then write down how the men of Nazareth tried to kill Jesus.

Talking

Imagine that you were a friend of Peter's mother-in-law. You heard the story of how she was made well. Now tell the story to an imaginary friend. Try and put in as much background detail as possible.

Illustration

Draw a picture showing the crowds of sick people and their friends, outside Peter's house.

— 9 —

The First Disciples

To help him in his work and to be his friends, Jesus chose twelve men who were called disciples. The word 'disciple' means a learner or follower. The first men to be called by Jesus were fishermen.

One day Jesus was walking by the Sea of Galilee when he saw two men. They were Simon Peter and his brother Andrew, and they were fishing. They stood in the shallow water not far from the shore, with their cast-nets. These nets had weights round the edge. When the fisher cast his net the weights made it sink and the fish were caught under the net. (See picture, p.25.)

Jesus spoke to Simon Peter and Andrew

'Come with me!' he said, 'and I will teach you how to catch men.' At once they left their nets and went with Jesus.

A little farther on Jesus saw two more brothers, James and John, mending their nets. These nets were much bigger than the cast-nets and were dragged through the water by a boat. At times two boats worked together, one at each end of the net.

James and John were in their boat with their father and some servants. Jesus called out to them and they too, as Peter and Andrew had done, left all and went with him.

Fishermen at work with a cast-net and fishing boat.

Later on, in the town of Capernaum, Jesus chose another disciple. He was named Matthew and he was a publican. 'Publican' is the name for a tax-collector. These men were hated by the Jews because they worked for the Romans. When they collected the taxes they often took more than the right money. This extra money went into their own pockets. It was no wonder that they were hated by the other Jews. When Jesus called Matthew from his table (see picture, p.14), he left what he was doing at once, just as the fishermen had done, and went with Jesus.

After this Matthew gave a great feast for Jesus. Many of his friends, other publicans, were there. The Pharisees, who were leaders of the Jewish religion, were shocked at what they saw. What was Jesus, this great teacher, doing with these hated tax-collecters? But Jesus had an answer for them.

'I have not come to help the people who think that they are

good [these were the Pharisees], but to help the sinners [these were the publicans]'.

Your turn now . . .

Research and discussion

Discuss the following with your friends and teachers.
a) Being a disciple was very difficult.
b) The disciples were different kinds of men.
c) Jesus mixed with sinners.

Thinking and writing

Imagine you are a newspaper reporter who just happens to come upon the scene when Jesus was recruiting his first disciples – the four fishermen.

Write a vivid newspaper report of this event. Give it a headline and include in your report as much background detail as possible.

Note

a) Make a list of the names of all the disciples. You can find them in Mark, Chapter 3, verses 16–19.
b) Pharisees, publicans – what do these words mean? Write them in your book.

―― 10 ――

A Miracle in a House

One day Jesus was preaching in a house in Capernaum. It may have been Peter's house. The room was full of people who had crowded in to be near to Jesus. Others, outside the door, tried to get near enough to hear what Jesus was saying.

Then four men came along carrying their friend on a sort of stretcher. This friend was paralysed and could not come to Jesus by himself. But because of the great crowd the men were not able to get into the house. They were not to be put off. They took their sick friend up the stairs outside the house and laid him down on the flat roof. (See picture, p.27.) There they began to think what they could do next.

A flat-roofed house in Palestine.

The only way to get to Jesus was through the roof. They began to make a hole. This was easy for them to do as the roof was made from sticks and sun-dried mud. It could soon be put right again. As soon as the hole was big enough they let down their friend at the feet of Jesus. When Jesus saw the faith of the four men he said some strange words to the sick man.

'Son,' he said, 'your sins are forgiven.' People in those days thought that illness was caused by sin. Jesus was telling this man that he had no need to worry about his sins: God would forgive them.

Some of the men in the room were Pharisees and scribes. The Pharisees, as we have read, were leaders of the Jewish religion and were very strict about the law: the scribes were lawyers. They did not like the words that Jesus had said.

'Who is this man to forgive sins?' they thought. 'Only God can do that.'

Jesus knew what was in their minds and he asked them why they were thinking like this. Then he asked them which was easier for him to say: 'Your sins are forgiven', or 'Take up your bed and walk'. Jesus turned again to the sick man.

'Get up!' he told him. 'Pick up your bed and go home.'

At once the man got up, took up his bed and walked away. All the people were amazed at what they had seen.

'We never saw anything like this before,' they said.

Your turn now...

Research and writing

Answer each of the following questions in a sentence.

a) What was the room like in which Jesus was talking?
b) Why was it impossible for the four friends to get near him?
c) What was wrong with the sick man?
d) Where did the friends take him?
e) How did they get him to Jesus?
f) Were all the people in the room friendly towards Jesus?
g) Who were the scribes?
h) What did everybody think when the sick man walked away?

Drama

Think about these things: the jostling crowds; the heat; the noise; the conversation; the sudden hole in the roof; the determination of the friends; the miracle.

Now, with a partner, act out the drama as if you were two of the people in the crowd.

— 11 —

Jesus makes Enemies

In the story of the man who was healed when his friends let him down through the roof of a house (Chapter 10), we read how Jesus upset some of the Pharisees when he said that he could forgive sins. Two things were to happen soon after this which made more enemies for Jesus.

One Sabbath day, Jesus and his disciples were walking along a path which led through a field of corn. The disciples were hungry, and they picked some of the corn that grew at the side of the path. There was nothing wrong in doing this, but some Pharisees who saw it said that they were doing work on the Sabbath day. It was against the law to do any work on the Sabbath.

The disciples picked corn from the side of the path.

But Jesus had an answer for them. He told them what David had done many years ago. He and his men, hungry and tired, had gone into the Temple and had taken the bread from the altar, bread that only the priests were allowed to eat. Now David was a great hero of the Jews, and they did not like to think that he had done any wrong. So the Pharisees could not argue any more with Jesus for what his disciples had done when they were hungry.

Again on a Sabbath day, Jesus went into a synagogue. In this synagogue there was a man with a paralysed hand. The men who were there watched Jesus, to see if he would heal this man on the Sabbath day. If he did so, then they would say that it was work, and against the law. Jesus saw the man and told him to stand up, and then he turned to the people around him. He knew very well what was in their minds.

'Is it right,' he asked them, 'to do good on the Sabbath day, or to do evil, to save life, or to kill?' There was, of course, only one answer to his question, but no one said anything. This made

Jesus very angry with them.

'Stretch out your hand!' he told the man. At once he did so, and the hand that had been useless and withered was well again, like the other.

At this, the enemies of Jesus went out to plot against him, to think how they could kill him.

Your turn now . . .

Research and discussion

Using the passage for help, discuss the following points with your friends and teacher.

a) In what way did Jesus make enemies?

b) Could Jesus answer his enemies' accusations?

c) Why do you think the Pharisees wanted to make trouble for Jesus?

Talking

'What did Jesus say?'

Imagine you were asked this question about how Jesus told the story of David and the bread on the alter. Then tell the story in your own words. The following words might help you:

hungry – tired – desperate – wondered – dared – necessary – forgiveness

Note

Read Mark, Chapter 3, verse 4. Write out the question that Jesus asked in the synagogue.

—— 12 ——

Jesus heals a Leper

One day a leper came to Jesus. Leprosy was a disease for which there was no cure. All lepers had to leave their homes and to live outside of towns and villages, away from all other people. But this leper had faith that Jesus was able to heal him. He came and knelt in front of Jesus.

'Lord, if you want to, you can heal me,' he said.

Jesus was sorry for the man. He put out his hand and touched him.

'I will heal you,' he said.

The pool of Bethesda had five porches.

At once the man's leprosy was gone.

Jesus had broken the law by touching the man. It was so easy to catch the disease by touching a leper. But by doing this Jesus showed that he had no fear of leprosy. Then he sent the man to show himself to the priest. He was the only man in the town who could say that the leper was well again, and let him come back to live with other people. Jesus told the man not to say anything about what he had done for him. But the man was so full of joy that he had to tell the people whom he met. So Jesus could not go into the towns or villages without crowds coming to see the man who had helped a leper.

One feast day, Jesus was in Jerusalem. He came to a place named Beth-es-da, where there was a pool with five porches around it. In these porches lay the blind, the lame, and many other sick people. They were waiting for the water to move. From time to time, it was said, an angel came to ripple the water, and the first sick person to go into the water after this was healed.

In one of the porches lay a man who had been ill for thirty-eight years. Jesus knew that this man had been there for a long time, and spoke to him.

'Do you want to be made well again?' he asked.

'Sir,' said the man, 'when the water in the pool is moved, I have nobody to put me into the water. While I am going, someone gets there before me.'

'Get up!' said Jesus. 'Take up your bed, and walk.'

At once the man was healed. He picked up his bed and went away, full of joy.

Your turn now . . .

Writing

I In Chapter 12 each of the following is important to the story. Write a few sentences about each.
   a) The leper.
   b) The Pool at Beth-es-da.
   c) The man who had been ill for thirty-eight years.

2 Write down the meaning of the following words. Use a dictionary where necessary:

leprosy   faith   lame   porches

Drama

Prepare a three part drama about Jesus and the leper. Think of the parts as follows:
a) before the leper met Jesus;
b) what happened when they met;
c) afterwards.
Think carefully about such things as: resignation, hope, fear, disbelief, joy, relief, gratitude. Try and make your dramatic work reflect these things.

The Centurion's Servant

In the city of Capernaum lived a Roman centurion. This man was an officer of the Roman army, and his name shows that he was in charge of a hundred men. The Romans were not often friends of the Jews, but this man had many friends among the leading Jews. They told Jesus that the centurion had been very good to their nation, and had even built a synagogue for them to worship in. It was clear that the Jews wanted Jesus to help this man.

The centurion had a servant of whom he was very fond. The servant was lying at home, very ill, and his master had come to Jesus to ask if he would heal him.

'I will come and heal him,' said Jesus.

But the centurion told Jesus that he was not worthy to take

The centurion came to Jesus and asked him to heal his servant.

him into his house.

'I give orders to my men,' he said, 'and they do what I say. You need only to give the order, and my servant will be well again.'

Jesus was amazed at the faith of this man. He turned to the people and told them that he had never seen such faith, even among his own people, the Jews. Then he spoke to the centurion.

'Go home,' he said, 'and it will be as you have believed.' And his servant was healed at that very moment.

Not far from Capernaum was the city of Nain. One day, Jesus came to Nain just as a funeral was coming through the gates of the city. The dead man was the only son of a widow woman. When he saw her, Jesus felt very sorry for this woman, and came up to her. He stopped the men who were carrying her dead son, and then he turned to the dead man.

'Young man, get up!' he said.

At once, the dead man sat up, and spoke. His mother was able to take him home again with her, full of joy at the wonderful miracle that Jesus had done for her.

Your turn now . . .

Writing

Find the facts and write down the answers in sentences.
a) What evidence is there that the centurion was a friend of Jews?
b) What evidence is there that the centurion was a kind and caring man?
c) Why was Jesus sorry for the widow at Nain?
d) What happened when Jesus stopped the funeral?

Discussion

With your friends and teacher discuss the following:
   The centurion was one of the most remarkable people we hear about in the stories of Jesus.

What were the questions?

The *answers* which follow could be written in reply to certain *questions*. Write down what you think each question was. (Use the same letter as its answer.)
a) He commanded one hundred men.

in the stern of the boat. Full of fear, the disciples woke him up.

'Master,' they cried, 'save us, or we shall die.'

Jesus stood up, and spoke. 'Peace, be still!' he said.

All at once the wind stopped blowing, and the sea was calm once more. Then Jesus turned to his disciples, and asked them why they had such little faith. They looked at one another.

'What kind of man is this?' they asked. 'Even the wind and the sea obey him.'

The next story belongs to a day on which Jesus, by a miracle, fed five thousand people. We shall read about this in Chapter 16.

After this wonderful meal, Jesus sent his disciples back to their boat, to sail home across the Sea of Galilee. He himself sent the crowds away and then went alone to pray. When he was ready to go, the ship was far out at sea, tossed by great waves. The sail had been rolled up, as the wind was against them. The disciples rowed hard, but they were not able to move forward.

Then Jesus came to them, walking on the water. The disciples were very frightened. They thought that Jesus was a spirit. Then he spoke.

'It is I,' he said. 'Do not be afraid.'

Peter cried out to him: 'Lord, let me come to you on the water.'

Jesus told him to come, and he walked on the water to go to Jesus. Then Peter looked at the water at his feet, grew afraid, and lost his faith. At once he began to sink.

'Lord, save me,' he cried.

Jesus took Peter by the hand and led him back to the boat. As soon as they were in the boat the wind dropped and the sea was calm. Very soon they were safe and sound at the other side.

Your turn now . . .

Research and writing

a) Read Mark, Chapter 4, verse 39. Write in your own words how Jesus calmed the storm.

b) Read Mark, Chapter 4, verse 41. Write what the disciples said to each other.

c) Read Matthew, Chapter 14, verses 28–32. Why did Peter begin to sink?

b) 'There is no need for you to come,' he said.
c) He was amazed at the faith of the centurion.
d) 'Go home, and it will be as you have believed.'

— 14 —

Two Stories of the Sea

Jesus had been talking to great crowds all the day. When evening came, the disciples took Jesus in a boat across the Sea of Galilee. They had gone only a short way when a great storm arose. Such storms often came very suddenly on the Sea of Galilee.

The waves were so huge that the water began to fill the boat. The disciples tried hard to keep the water down, but it soon seemed that the boat must sink. All this time Jesus was asleep,

The ship was far out at sea, tossed by great waves.

Work with a partner on the following:

Imagine you are one of the disciples in the boat during the second storm. You are now saved, but you were terrified when you were rowing into the storm. You saw Jesus approach; you saw what happened to Peter; you experienced the peace and calm Jesus brought.

Work out a conversation you have with a friend about these things. Tape-record it if you can.

—— 15 ——

Jairus' Daughter

Jairus' daughter was dying. Jairus, who was a ruler of the synagogue, came to ask Jesus if he would come and heal her. Jesus was always ready to help people in need, and he set off to heal the girl.

In the crowd that went with Jesus there was a woman who had been very ill for twelve years. She had been to many doctors, and she had spent all her money in trying to find a cure. But, so far, no one had been able to help her in any way. Then she saw Jesus.

'If I can just touch his clothes,' she said to herself, 'then I shall be well again.'

She pushed through the crowd until she was just near enough to put out her hand and touch Jesus. At once she was well again. But Jesus stopped and turned round.

'Who touched me?' he asked.

The disciples were amazed at his words. A great crowd was pushing around Jesus. How could he know that anyone had touched him? When the woman knew that he had felt her touch she fell down at his feet, afraid of what she had done. But Jesus spoke kindly to her.

'Your faith has made you well again,' he said.

Just then, someone came from Jairus' house to tell him that his little girl was dead. There was no need for him to worry Jesus any more. But Jesus told him not to be afraid, only to believe. Jesus took with him Peter, James, and John, and went to the house. There they found a crowd of people, all weeping.

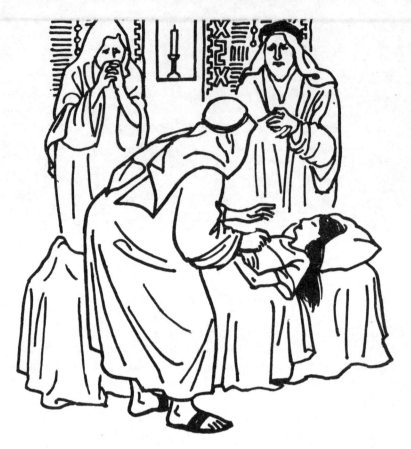

'Little girl,' said Jesus, 'get up.'

'Why do you weep?' he asked. 'The little girl is not dead, she is only asleep.'

The people laughed at these words of Jesus, for they were quite sure that the girl was dead. But Jesus sent them away. He took the three disciples, and the mother and father of the girl, and went to where she lay, still and white.

'Little girl,' he said to her, 'get up!'

At once, to the great joy of her mother and father, she got up. Jesus knew that she would be hungry, and he told her parents to give her something to eat.

Your turn now . . .

Research and discussion

With your friends and teacher discuss the following.

a) The modesty and faith of the sick woman.

Illustration

Paint a colourful picture of the crowds around Jesus when he got the message about Jairus' daughter. Leave out the figures of Jesus and the sick woman.

Draw and paint these two figures on thicker paper or card. Then stick them onto your painting so that they stand out amongst the crowd.

Research

How old was Jairus' daughter? Read Mark, Chapter 5, from verse 35 until you find out.

—————— 16 ——————

The Feeding of the Five Thousand

Because of the great crowds who wanted to hear Jesus or to be healed by him, Jesus and his disciples did not have much time alone. One day, they sailed over the Sea of Galilee, to a lonely spot, so that they could get away from the crowds. But the people saw them go away in their boat, and went round the lake. In this way many of them reached the other side before Jesus. When, at last, he got there, he felt sorry for these people, and began to talk to them and to heal those who were sick.

Later in the day, the disciples told Jesus that the crowds must be hungry as they had nothing with them to eat. They would have to go to the nearest villages to buy food.

'You give them something to eat,' said Jesus.

'Why, even if we go and buy two hundred pennyworth of bread, that would not be enough for all these people,' said Philip. Then Andrew came up and spoke to Jesus:

'Here is a boy with five small loaves and two fishes,' he said 'but what good are they among so many people?'

'Make the people sit down!' said Jesus.

The five loaves and two fishes.

There were five thousand men there, as well as some women and children. They sat down in groups on the grass and waited to see what Jesus was going to do. Jesus took the loaves and the fishes and blessed them. Then he gave them to his disciples and told them to share the food among the crowd. They did as he told them, and when all of them had eaten enough they collected the bits that were left. They were amazed to find that there was enough to fill twelve baskets.

When they saw this great miracle, the five thousand men said:

'We must have this man for our leader.'

They even tried to make him their king. But Jesus was a man of peace. He did not want to be the kind of king who would lead the people to war against the Romans.

So Jesus sent the crowds away, while his disciples set off in their boat across the Sea of Galilee once more. We have read, in Chapter 14, what happened to them on their way home.

Your turn now . . .

Research and writing

Answer each of the following questions with a sentence.
a) Why did Jesus have little time to spend alone?
b) What was the purpose of the trip across the Sea of Galilee?

c) How did the crowds reach the 'lonely spot' before Jesus?
d) Where did the people expect to get food?
e) What did Andrew discover?
f) How many men were in the crowd?
g) How much food was left after everybody had eaten?
h) What did the people want Jesus to be?
i) What do you think they wanted him to do?

Reference

Verses 19 and 20 in Matthew, Chapter 14, are very important in telling this story. Write them out in your book. Make this look interesting by putting what you think is a suitable border round it. Think carefully about what things you might show in your border.

—— 17 ——

Peter's Wonderful Answer

To get away from the crowds and from his enemies, Jesus went far away to the north. He had a lot to teach his disciples so that they could carry on his work when he had gone. At last they came to a place named Caesarea Philippi. Here Jesus asked his disciples two questions.

First he asked them, 'Who do people say that I am?' Their answer was that people said that he was one of the prophets who had come back to life. (Remember that the prophets were men chosen by God to be his messengers to his people.) Some said that he was the great old prophet Elijah, others said that he was John the Baptist.

Then Jesus asked them, 'But who do you say that I am?' At once Peter replied. 'You are the Christ, the Son of God.'

Jesus told his disciples that they must not tell anyone about this. If the people heard that he was the Christ they would crowd round him again and his enemies would try to put him to death at once.

From this time Jesus began to tell his disciples how he must go back to Jerusalem, where he would be arrested and put to death. But on the third day, he told them, he would rise again from the dead. The disciples were very sorry to hear Jesus say this. Peter even tried to stop him from going back to

The Transfiguration of Jesus.

Jerusalem. But Jesus told Peter that he must not tempt him. It was God's will that Jesus must die and he had to do God's will.

A few days later Jesus took Peter, James and John up into the hills, where a strange thing happened. We call this the Transfiguration: this word means a change of appearance. Jesus' face shone like the sun and his robe was dazzling white. The three disciples could hardly bear to look at him. In the brightness they saw two men talking with Jesus. They were Moses, the great leader who brought the Children of Israel out of Egypt, and Elijah, one of the great prophets.

Then a cloud shut out their view and they heard God's voice:
'This is my beloved Son in whom I am well pleased: hear him!'
The disciples were afraid and hid their faces. When they looked up again they saw Jesus alone. As they came down the hill they wondered about what they had seen. They did not understand it, but they knew that they had been with Jesus when something wonderful had taken place.

Your turn now...

Research and writing

The following words are important in this chapter. Write a sentence about each.
a) Caesarea Philippi
b) Prophet
c) Elijah
d) Disciples
e) Jerusalem
f) Peter
g) Transfiguration

Discussion

Discuss the following points with your friends and teacher.
a) Why did Jesus travel far away to the north?
b) Why did Jesus have to prepare his disciples for the future?
c) How did the disciples react to his warning?
d) Could his disciples fully understand all that was happening to Jesus?

—— 18 ——

Jesus heals a Boy

When Jesus and his three disciples came down the hill after the Transfiguration, they found a great crowd of people at the foot of the hill. In the middle of the crowd were the other disciples, talking with some scribes. These scribes were Jewish lawyers, and they often found fault with things that Jesus said or did.

A man came to Jesus from the crowd. His son was deaf and dumb, and he suffered from fits.

'Master,' the man said to Jesus, 'I brought my son to your disciples, but they could not heal him.'

'Bring him to me!' said Jesus.

As the father brought his son to Jesus, the boy fell down in a fit. Jesus asked the man how long the boy had been like this. The father told him that he had been like this since he was a child. In his fits he often fell into the water or into the fire.

— 43 —

The father brought his son to Jesus.

'If you can do anything,' he said, 'have pity, and help us.'

'If you can believe,' said Jesus, 'anything is possible.'

With tears in his eyes, the father told Jesus that he did believe. Then Jesus took the boy and healed him.

Later the disciples asked Jesus, 'Why couldn't we heal the boy?'

'Because you did not have enough faith,' he said,. 'You can only cast out such evil spirits if you have faith. Faith can even move mountains.' This was an old Jewish way of saying that faith can do the impossible.

After this, Jesus and his disciples came back to the town of Capernaum. Some tax-collectors came up to Peter, and asked him, 'Does your Master pay tax money?'

'Yes!' said Peter. This tax money was used to pay for the services in the Temple at Jerusalem.

When Peter came to Jesus in the house, Jesus told him that they must not upset the tax-collectors by not paying the tax.

Then he told him to do a strange thing.

'Go to the sea,' he said, 'and the first fish that you shall catch will have a coin in its mouth. It will be just enough to pay the tax for you and me.'

Your turn now...

Research and writing

Read Mark, Chapter 9, verses 23–24. Now write out:
a) the words which Jesus said to the father of the boy;
b) the father's reply.

Writing

Imagine that you were one of the crowd at the bottom of the hill. You notice the scribes who are against Jesus as well as those people who seek his help.

Try to imagine the scene before Jesus arrives. Different people are expecting different things; the atmosphere is at fever-pitch. Try and describe this as vividly as you can in one paragraph.

Drama

Act out the scene of Peter catching the fish with the coin in its mouth. Try to show exactly how you think he felt when this happened.

—— 19 ——

Jesus in Jericho

On his way back to Jerusalem, Jesus had to pass through Galilee and Samaria. One day he came near to a village, and ten men who were lepers saw him. They called out to him:

'Jesus, have mercy on us.' Jesus was sorry for them and he told them to go to the priests. On the way they found that they had all been healed. But out of the ten only one came back to thank Jesus. This man was not a Jew but a Samaritan, a man from Samaria.

At last Jesus came to Jericho. Near the city was a blind man who sat by the side of the road to beg. He was called

Zacchaeus climbed a fig tree to see Jesus.

Bartimaeus. This was not really his name, but means 'son of Timaeus'. When this blind man heard the shouts of the people who were with Jesus he asked what was going on. He was told that Jesus was going by and he began to shout out.

'Jesus, have mercy on me,' he called. The people told him to be quiet, but he only shouted out more. When Jesus heard him he stopped and sent for him.

'What do you want me to do for you?' Jesus asked the man.

'Lord, I want my sight,' he said.

At once, because the blind man had faith, Jesus healed him, and he went along with Jesus and his disciples.

In the city of Jericho lived a man named Zacchaeus (*Za-key-us*). He was a chief tax-collector and he was very rich. When he heard that Jesus was coming he tried hard to see him. But he was a very small man and he could not see for the great crowd of people. He ran along the road and climbed a fig (sycamore) tree. Here he could see Jesus as he went by. But when Jesus came to the tree he stopped and looked up.

'Hurry and come down, Zacchaeus,' he said. 'I want to stay at your house to-day.'

Gladly Zacchaeus came down and took Jesus to his home. Many people in the crowd did not like this. They began to say that Jesus should not stay with a sinful man like Zacchaeus. You will remember from the story of Matthew in Chapter 9 that the Jews hated the tax-collectors, as they worked for the Romans.

Zacchaeus was a changed man when Jesus left. He promised to give half of his money to the poor. To those from whom he had taken too much tax, he promised to give back four times as much as he had taken.

Your turn now . . .

Research and writing

Answer the following questions in sentences.
a) Where did Jesus meet the ten lepers?
b) Where did the leper come from who came back to thank Jesus?
c) Why didn't Bartimaeus know what was going on at first?
d) What was the name of Jericho's chief tax-collector?
e) What do we know about Zacchaeus's appearance?
f) Where did Jesus stay in Jericho?
g) Why were some people annoyed because Jesus stayed there?

Discussion

With your friends and teacher discuss the following statements:
'Zaccheaus was a curious man.'
'Events can change people's lives.'
'Actions speak louder than words.'

Illustration

Look at the following diagram. Put it in your book but replace all the words with drawings.

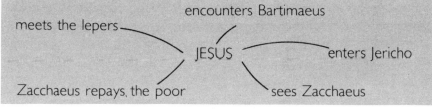

Jesus restores Lazarus to Life

At Bethany, not far from Jerusalem, Jesus had some very good friends. He often used to visit them when he was near to their village. When Jesus came to their house one day, Mary was quiet and sat at his feet to hear what he had to say. But her sister, Martha, was too busy with the meal to stop and talk. There is a wonderful story about these two friends of Jesus and their brother, Lazarus.

Lazarus was very ill and his sisters sent a message to Jesus. But by the time that Jesus came to Bethany, Lazarus was dead. For four days his body had lain in a rock tomb. (See picture.) When Martha heard that Jesus was near she left Mary in the house and went out to meet him.

'Lord,' she said, 'if you had been here my brother would not

Jesus called out in a loud voice: 'Lazarus, come out!'

have died.'

Jesus sent her home to bring Mary to him. When she came Mary said the same words that Martha had said to Jesus. She was weeping as she spoke and Jesus wept with her. When they saw this the people began to say that this man, who healed the sick, could have saved Lazarus from death.

Then they came to the tomb. It was a cave in the rock with a stone over the opening.

'Take away the stone,' said Jesus, and soon this was done. Then Jesus prayed aloud to God. He did this so that the people who stood by, when they saw the miracle, would know that Jesus had been sent by God. After this he called out in a loud voice:

'Lazarus, come out!'

All the people stared at the open cave. To the joy of his sisters and all their friends in the village, the man who had been dead came out from the mouth of the cave. He was still wearing the special clothes in which he had been buried. When these clothes had been untied Lazarus was able to go home with Mary and Martha. The house which had been a place of sadness was once more full of joy.

Many of the people were very happy to have seen such a great miracle, but the priests, when they heard of it, made up their minds that they must get rid of Jesus.

Your turn now . . .

Research and discussion

With your friends and teacher discuss the following.
a) Why do you think Jesus enjoyed going to Bethany?
b) Why did the priests want to get rid of Jesus?

Drama

Act out a scene showing Jesus and the disciples arriving at their friends' house in Bethany after a long journey. Think about the following before preparing your drama: How did they travel?   What were the roads like?   What would travellers need when they arrived?   How might they be greeted?

Writing

a) Write down the meaning of the following words. Use a dictionary where necessary:
tomb   miracle   cave
b) Imagine that you could travel back in time to see Jesus call Lazarus from the tomb. Write about what you see, hear, feel, smell, touch. Describe how the other people respond to the miracle.

—— 21 ——

Jesus enters Jerusalem

At last Jesus and his disciples came near to Jerusalem, where they were to hold the Feast of the Passover. Remember that this was a very great Feast, which reminded the Jews of the day when they came out of Egypt, many years before. At the Mount of Olives, so called because of the many olive trees that grew there, Jesus called two of his disciples. He told them to go to a village nearby.

'There you will find a colt tied up, which nobody has ever ridden,' he told them. 'Untie him and bring him back to me.' The colt was, of course, a young ass or donkey. Jesus told them that they might be asked why they were taking the colt. Then they were to say, 'The Lord needs him,' and they would be able to take him at once.

The two disciples came to the village and found the colt, just as Jesus had told them. It was tied up outside a house, where two roads met. Some men asked why they were taking him, and they gave the answer that Jesus had told them. The men let them go on their way.

They brought the colt to Jesus, and put some cloaks on his back for a seat. Then Jesus sat on him, and they set out along the road to the great city. The crowd with Jesus spread their coats, and leaves from the palm trees, along the road, as a carpet for him to ride over. He was coming to Jerusalem as a king, a king of peace. All the people were shouting.

'Hosanna!' they cried. 'Blessed is the one who comes in the Name of the Lord.'

So Jesus rode in triumph into the city, and came to the Temple. By the time that he had looked around, the day was

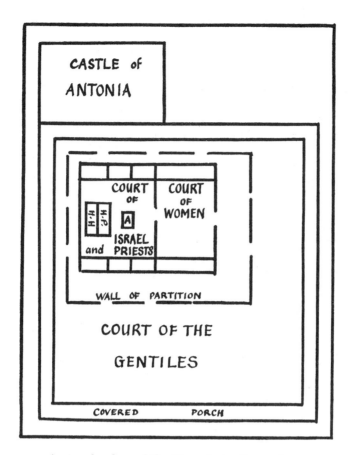

A simple plan of the Temple in Jerusalem.
H.H. = the Holy of Holies.   H.P. = The Holy Place   A. = The Altar.

he turned over the tables of the men who were changing money; and he would not let anyone carry things through the Temple courtyard. Nobody tried to stop him, for they must have known that it was wrong to use God's House in this way. Even the priests were afraid of starting a riot among the people. The Roman castle was next to the Temple (see diagram), and they did not want the Roman soldiers to have to come down and stop a riot: they might even stop the Feast of the Passover.

Then Jesus spoke out: 'My house is a house of prayer for all nations: but you have made it a den of thieves.'

He called them thieves because many of them were cheats. Some of them cheated in changing money; some sold sick animals in place of perfect ones, for sacrifice.

Many of the people were glad to see what Jesus had done. The Gentiles were full of joy. But the priests were very angry, and they made up their minds that they must get rid of Jesus as soon as they could.

Your turn now...

Research and writing

Write about the scene in the Temple. You can report it in your own words, or you can describe it as if you had been there.

Try and give a *vivid* description of all that happened. Use the passage and the plan of the Temple to help you.

Drama

Act out two dramas.
a) What the people who approved of Jesus' actions said and did.
b) What his enemies said and did.

Notes
Write out in your book:
a) the meaning of GENTILE;
b) Mark, Chapter 11, verse 18.

—— 23 ——

The Tax Money

During the last week of Jesus' life, he spent much of his time in the Temple, preaching and healing the people. His enemies tried hard to arrest and to kill him. But they were always afraid that the crowd might turn on them. One day some of them tried to catch Jesus with a question. These men were Pharisees and Herodians. The Pharisees were very religious men: the Herodians were followers of King Herod, and they tried to keep friendly with the Romans. These two groups hated one another, yet they came together to try to catch their enemy, Jesus.

When they came to Jesus, they said:

'We know that you care only for the truth, and that you are not afraid of any man. Is it right for us to pay taxes to Caesar or not?' Caesar was, of course, the Roman Emperor.

Jesus' enemies knew that he could not say 'Yes' or 'No' to

their question, without getting into trouble. If he said that it was right to pay tax to the Romans, a lot of the Jews would not like it, for they hated the Romans: if he said that it was wrong, then the Romans might arrest him.

Roman and Jewish coins.
Above: *Roman gold coin.* Below: *A Jewish silver shekel.*
Note: *Both sides of each coin are shown.*

But Jesus knew that these men were trying to catch him with their question. He told them to bring him a penny. When they had done this he spoke to them:

'Whose head is on this coin, and whose name is this?' asked Jesus. His enemies told him that the penny had Caesar's head and name on it.

'Then give to Caesar what belongs to him,' said Jesus, 'and give to God what is his.'

There was nothing that his enemies could say or do after this. They did not dare to arrest Jesus, as many of the people were pleased with his clever answer.

Your turn now...

Research and writing

Read the passage again and say what you know about each of the following:
a) Pharisees
b) Herodians
c) Caesar
d) Penny

Discussion

With your friends and teacher discuss the following.
a) The Pharisees and the Herodians came together for one purpose.
b) Why Jesus asked for a penny.
c) Jesus' clever answer.
d) Why his enemies dared not arrest him.

Talking

With a partner work out the conversation which might have taken place between a Pharisee and a Herodian. Use the following words to help your thoughts: enemies – truce – reasons – money – disappointed – clever – wait.

—— 24 ——

Judas betrays Jesus

We have read how the enemies of Jesus were trying to arrest and to kill him. They wanted to do this before the Feast of the Passover began. But if they took Jesus while the crowds were there it might cause a riot, for he had many friends among the people. In this case the Roman soldiers would have to stop the riot, and they might even stop the Feast itself. The priests did not know that one of Jesus' own disciples was going to help them with their plans, and was going to betray Jesus to them.

One day, Jesus was in the house of a man named Simon the Leper in Bethany. He was not a leper now but might have been once, and so he had this name. While he was there, a woman came in with a box of ointment which she poured over Jesus' head, as if to anoint him. The ointment had cost a lot of money, and the disciples said that this was a waste. It could have been sold, and the money given to the poor.

Judas Iscariot, one of the twelve disciples, was there at this time. He was the man who looked after the disciples' money, and perhaps this waste upset him. It was soon after this that he went off to the priests to betray Jesus.

The priests were very glad to see Judas and hear what he had to say to them. Now they would be able to take Jesus quietly, away from the crowds, with the help of this disciple. They agreed to pay him thirty pieces of silver for what he was going to do.

As the time for the Feast of the Passover came near, the disciples asked Jesus where they were to eat the Passover meal. He sent two of them into Jerusalem.

'Go into the city,' he told the, 'and you will meet a man with a pitcher of water. Follow him to his house and ask where is the

The house with the Upper Room.

room for our meal.'

The disciples did as Jesus had said, and found the man quite easily. It was usually the work of women to carry water. They went to his house, and there they found a big upstairs room. Here they got ready for the Passover meal.

Your turn now . . .

Note
Write in your book JUDAS ISCARIOT. Iscariot means 'Man of Kerioth'.

Answer the following questions in sentences.
a) When did Jesus' enemies want to arrest him?
b) Who would have to stop any rioting?
c) What disease had Simon from Bethany suffered from?
d) What cost a lot of money?
e) Why were the priests glad to see Judas?
f) What was the price of the betrayal?
g) How did the disciples know where to go for the Passover meal?

Reading and finding out

Read Mark, Chapter 14, verse 5 and 13–15. Answer the following questions:
a) How much was the ointment worth?
b) What was the upstairs room like?

—— 25 ——

The Last Supper

In Chapter 24 we read how the disciples found the house where Jesus was to eat the Passover meal with them. They had made the Upper Room of the house ready, and in the evening Jesus came with the Twelve. This was to be the last meal that Jesus had with his disciples before his death. As they sat at the table, Jesus said a strange thing.

'One of you is going to betray me,' he said.

Jesus knew what Judas was going to do. When the disciples asked who it was, Jesus said that it was the one who dipped bread with him in the dish. It was Judas. Soon after this he went out to betray Jesus to the priests.

Then Jesus took one of the flat cakes of bread, broke it, and gave it to his disciples.

'Take this and eat it,' he said. 'It is my body.'

The bread and the wine at the Last Supper.

Then he took the cup of wine, and gave it to them, with these words:

'This is my blood, which is shed for many people.'

Jesus meant that he was going to give up his life, his body and his blood, for them and for all people. Ever since that time, Christians have taken the bread and wine, in memory of Jesus's death and this 'Last Supper', as it is called.

After supper was over, Jesus took a bowl of water and a towel, and he began to wash the feet of his disciples. This was work done by a servant, and Jesus was giving his disciples a lesson that they should be humble. If he, their Master, could wash their feet, then they should wash one another's feet.

'I have given you an example,' said Jesus, 'so that you can do the same as I have done.'

The disciples needed this lesson, for that very evening they had been arguing about which of them was the greatest.

The last thing they did in the Upper Room was to sing a hymn together. Then they went out into the night. They were going to a place which Jesus knew well, the Mount of Olives.

Your turn now . . .

Research and writing

The following are important in this chapter. Write at least one sentence about each:
a) Upper Room;
b) betray;
c) flat cake of bread;
d) bread and wine;
e) bowl of water;
f) servant;
g) arguing;
h) Mount of Olives.

Talking

Imagine you were one of the disciples. Describe in careful detail what happened at the Last Supper — don't forget to note that Judas left early.

Apart from describing events, describe also how you and your friends felt.

Prepare this talk very carefully and when you have finished, tape-record it if you can.

—— 26 ——

The Arrest of Jesus

On the Mount of Olives was a garden called the Garden of Gethsemane. Jesus had often come here with his disciples, and it was here that they came from the Upper Room.

As they went, Jesus told his disciples that they would all lose faith in him that night. Each one of them said that he would keep faith whatever might happen. Peter said that he was ready to go to prison or even to die for Jesus. Then Jesus spoke to Peter:

'This night, before the cock crows in the morning, you will deny three times that you know me.'

When they reached the Garden, Jesus took with him Peter, James and John. He told them to keep watch while he went on to pray. When he came back he found them all asleep.

'Could you not watch for one hour?' he asked Peter. Then he went away again to pray. Twice more he came back and found them asleep, for they were very tired.

As Jesus spoke to them the third time, a crowd of men came into the Garden, with swords and sticks and torches. They had come from the chief priests to arrest Jesus and Judas was at

While Jesus went to pray his disciples fell asleep.

their head. So that they could find Jesus in the dark, Judas had given them a sign:

'He is the one whom I shall greet with a kiss. Take him!' Judas had told them.

So Judas came up to Jesus and kissed him. At once the men who had come with him took hold of Jesus to lead him away.

But Peter drew a sword and struck out to help his Master. He cut off the ear of a servant of the High Priest. Jesus told Peter that he must put away his sword, and then he turned to the man who had been wounded and healed him. It was then that all the disciples left Jesus and ran away.

While all this was going on, a young man was watching. He had followed Jesus and his disciples to the Garden, with only a sheet wrapped around him. We think that he was John Mark, who had come from the house with the Upper Room. The soldiers took hold of him, but he was able to slip out of the sheet and run away.

So Jesus was led away by the men who had come to arrest him, and taken to the High Priest.

Your turn now . . .

Research and writing

Answer the following questions in sentences.
a) Where was the Garden of Gethsemane?
b) Which disciple said he was prepared to die for Jesus?
c) Did Jesus know what Peter would do after the arrest?
d) What did Peter, James and John do whilst Jesus prayed?
e) Who led the crowd of men with swords, sticks and torches?
f) How did the men know which of the group was Jesus?
g) Which disciple fought back?
h) Where was Jesus taken after the arrest?

Talking

Imagine you are a newspaper reporter for *Time and Space* magazine. You travel back to report the arrest of Jesus.

Write out what you are going to say. (Try to recapture the atmosphere of torch-lit darkness, Judas' signal, the noise and struggle of the arrest.)

Next tape-record your report. With some friends you might also be able to put in some sound-effects.

27

Peter denies Jesus

After his arrest in the Garden of Gethsemane, Jesus was taken to the palace of the High Priest. All his disciples had fled, but Peter came back and followed the crowd at a distance.

At the palace, the scribes and leaders of the people were with the High Priest. His enemies meant to put Jesus to death, but they were not able to find any way of doing this. There were many men who stood up to tell the things that Jesus had said and done, but none of them told the same story. The Jewish Law said that at least two of the witnesses must agree in what they

Peter was warming himself at the fire in the yard of the palace.

said. Even men who had been paid to tell lies about Jesus were not able to agree.

While all this was happening, Jesus said nothing at all. The High Priest grew angry, and at last he turned to Jesus.

'Are you the Christ, the Son of God?' he asked him.

'I am,' said Jesus.

At these words, all his enemies said that Jesus must die. No man could claim to be the Son of God. The men around him began to spit at him, to hit him, to cover his eyes and ask him to say who it was that struck him.

At this time, Peter was warming himself at the fire in the yard of the palace. Many of the High Priest's servants were there with him. One of the maids came up to Peter.

'You were one of those with Jesus of Nazareth,' she said.

'I don't know what you are talking about,' said Peter, and went out into the porch. There another maid said to the servants:

'This man was with Jesus of Nazareth.'

'I don't know this man,' said Peter.

Later, other servants said that they were sure that he was one of the disciples, for his way of speaking gave him away. At once, Peter began to swear that he was not a disciple.

It was then that Peter heard the cock crow. He remembered the words that Jesus had said to him, that he would deny him three times before the cock crew. When he knew what he had done, he went out and wept.

Your turn now . . .

Research and discussion

Discuss the following with your friends and teacher.
a) The effect of fear.
b) Gaining strength from weakness.

Writing

Write out two passages.
a) Imagine you were an eye-witness and describe what happened when Jesus was brought before the High Priest.
b) Imagine you were an eye-witness in the yard of the palace and describe how Peter behaved.

In both pieces of writing try to write just as if you were speaking to somebody.

Note

Write out the verse which tells how the High Priest's men treated Jesus. (Mark, Chapter 14, verse 65.)

28

Jesus before Pilate

In the morning, after he had been tried by the priests, Jesus was taken to Pontius Pilate, the Roman Governor. By Roman law

'Crucify him!' shouted the people.

the Jews could not put any man to death, so it had to be the Romans who killed him.

When Judas, who had betrayed Jesus, saw what was happening, he was very sorry for what he had done. He took the thirty pieces of silver to give them back to the priests. But the priests would have nothing to do with him. He had done what they wanted, and now they had no more use for him. There was only one thing for him to do: he went out and hanged himself.

So Jesus stood before Pilate, while his enemies told the Governor what he had said and done. Pilate was sure that Jesus had done no wrong, and he wanted to set him free. But Jesus had nothing to say in his defence. At last Pilate spoke to him.

'Are you the King of the Jews?' he asked.

'You say that I am,' was all that Jesus said.

Then Pilate found out that Jesus was from Galilee, in the north. This part of Palestine was ruled by King Herod. So Pilate sent Jesus to Herod, who was in Jerusalem for the Feast of the Passover. He hoped that this would save him from having to sentence Jesus himself.

Herod was glad to see Jesus. He had heard a lot about him, and he hoped that Jesus would do some miracle for him. But once more, Jesus had nothing to say. At last Herod and his men dressed Jesus in a royal robe, as King of the Jews, and sent him back to Pilate.

Once again Pilate tried to set Jesus free. He said that he would flog him and let him go. But the priests cried out that Jesus must die. They had persuaded the crowd to shout against Jesus, whose friends were too afraid to help him.

Then Pilate came to the people again. There was one more chance to free Jesus. Each year at the Feast of the Passover, Pilate set free one prisoner to please the Jews. He had a prisoner named Barabbas, who was in prison for revolt and murder. He would offer the people Jesus or Barabbas. Pilate spoke to the crowd.

'Shall I free the King of the Jews?' he asked. But the crowd shouted for Barabbas.

'What shall I do to the King of the Jews?' said Pilate.

'Crucify him!' shouted the people.

At last Pilate gave way to the Jews. To please them, he set Barabbas free, and sent Jesus away to be flogged and crucified.

Your turn now . . .

Research and writing

1 Answer each of the following with a sentence.
   a) Why couldn't the Jews put a man to death?
   b) What did Judas want to do with the thirty pieces of silver?
   c) Why did Pilate sent Jesus to Herod?
   d) Who persuaded the crowd to shout against Jesus?
   e) What was Pilate's last effort to free Jesus?

2 Write down the meaning of the following words. Use a

dictionary where necessary:

betrayed   sentence   defence   revolt   crucify

3 Imagine you are Pilate. You want to free Jesus but there are difficulties. Write an account of what you did at this time, how you felt, what worried you, what you tried to do. Begin your account with the words: 'It was the time of my life which I regretted most . . .

(Note: read Matthew, Chapter 27, verse 24.)

— 29 —

The Crucifixion

When Pilate gave his soldiers the order to crucify Jesus, they took him away. He was dressed in a royal robe, and a crown of long, sharp thorns was put on his head. Then they began to mock him:

'Hail! King of the Jews,' they cried, and knelt as if to worship him. They hit him and spit on him, as the priests had done before. Then he was flogged and dressed in his own clothes, and taken to be crucified. Weak from the flogging, Jesus was not able to carry his cross, and the Romans made a man named Simon carry it for him. So they came to Golgotha, where Jesus was to be crucified.

There Jesus was nailed to the cross, and the soldiers gambled for his clothes. On each side of Jesus was a thief, and over his head were the words, 'THE KING OF THE JEWS'. Even as he was put on the cross Jesus prayed for his enemies.

'Father, forgive them,' he said, 'for they do not know what they are doing.'

A few of Jesus' friends stood round the cross, but many of the people mocked him, and told him to save himself as he had saved so many other people.

'Save yourself, and come down from the cross!' they cried.

Even one of the thieves at his side asked him to save himself and them. But the other one stopped him.

'We are getting what we deserve,' he said, 'but this man has done no wrong.' Then he turned and spoke to Jesus: 'Jesus, remember me when you come into your kingdom.'

'Today,' said Jesus, 'you will be with me in Heaven.'

The hours went by. From noon until three in the afternoon there was a great darkness over the land. And then Jesus died. The Roman centurion, who stood at the foot of the cross, spoke out:

'Truly, this man was the Son of God,' he said.

Jesus was crucified between two thieves.

That evening, a man called Joseph came to Pilate and asked for the body of Jesus. When Pilate knew that he was dead, he let Joseph take his body. He laid it quietly in his own tomb, cut out of the rock, and rolled a large stone across the opening.

Because the priests feared that the disciples would steal the body and then say that Jesus had risen from the dead, they put a guard on the tomb.

Research and discussion

With your friends and teacher dicuss the following.
a) Why was Jesus dressed in royal clothes?
b) Why did the soldiers gamble for his clothes?
c) Why did the priests put a guard outside the tomb?

Writing

Write down the meaning of the following words. Use a dictionary where necessary:
mock   flogged   centurion

Talking

Work with a partner. Imagine that one of you is an interviewer and the other is the Roman centurion who stood at the foot of the cross.
Work out what questions might be asked – and possible replies.
Present your interview to the rest of the class and ask for their opinions about it.

Note
Write in your book: GOLGOTHA – a hill shaped like a skull.

— 30 —

Jesus rises from the Dead

Very early on Sunday morning, the third day after Jesus had been crucified, some women came to the tomb to anoint his body with spices. They had not been able to do this when his body was laid in the tomb, for it had been late in the day. The next day had been the Sabbath when no one must work. But now the Sabbath was over and they could do this last service for the one they loved.

As they came near they wondered how they could roll away the large stone from the opening of the tomb. But when they got there they found, to their amazement, that the stone was already moved away. There they saw an angel who told them

Jesus said to her, 'Mary!'

that Jesus had risen from the dead and that they must go and
tell his disciples.

When Peter and John heard this news they ran to the tomb.
John was a young man and got there first. He stood outside and
looked in. But when Peter got there he went right into the tomb
and John followed him. They saw the clothes in which Jesus
had been buried, but there was no sign of Jesus himself. They
knew that what the women had told them was true. Jesus was
alive again.

After Peter and John had gone Mary Magdalene stood alone
near the tomb. We think that Mary had this name because she
came from the town of Magdala. She was a woman whom Jesus
had healed. As she stood there she was weeping. Then she heard
a voice speaking to her:

'Woman, why are you crying?'

Through her tears Mary saw a man standing near the tomb.
She thought that he must be the gardener and she told him that

she was crying because the body of Jesus had been taken away.
Then Jesus, for it was he, spoke one word to her.

'Mary!' he said.

At once Mary knew that he was the Lord.

'Master!' she cried, and fell at his feet.

Jesus told her to go and tell his disciples that he was alive
again. So Mary went to Jerusalem and told the disciples how
Jesus had spoken to her.

Your turn now . . .

Research and writing

Write at least one sentence about each of the following:
a) Sabbath;
b) 'the stone was already moved away';
c) 'the great news';
d) Mary Magdalene;
e) Jerusalem.

Illustration

Draw a dramatic picture of Mary Magdalene giving the 'great news'
to Peter and John. Try to make their faces and hands show their
feelings.

Notes

a) What did the angel say to the women? See Matthew, Chapter
28, verses 5–7.
b) What does the word RABBONI mean? Find out by reading
John, Chapter 20, verses 15–16.

—— 31 ——

The Road to Emmaus

It was the same day that Jesus had risen from the dead and had
spoken to Mary Magdalene near the tomb. Two disciples were
going home from Jerusalem to the village of Emmaus. We know
the name of one of them: he was Cleopas. The other one may
have been his wife. As they walked along they were talking

Jesus took some bread, blessed it and broke it.

sadly about the death of Jesus.

As they talked Jesus himself came up to them, but they did
not know him. He asked them what they were talking about
and why they were so sad. Cleopas told him all that had
happened to Jesus and how they had heard the amazing news
that he was alive again. Then Jesus began to talk about himself
and how all these things had to happen, for they were the will of
God.

Soon they came to Emmaus. It was nearly evening and the
two disciples asked Jesus to stay the night with them.

'Stay with us,' they said, 'for the day is nearly over.' The three
of them went into the house.

As they sat down to eat Jesus took some bread, blessed it and
broke it, and then gave it to the disciples. At once they knew
who he was, but Jesus vanished from their sight.

The two disciples had only just come from Jerusalem but they
set off again for the city to tell the other disciples the great
news. They found eleven, with some others, in the Upper Room.
With joy they told them all that had happened on the road to

Emmaus, and how they had known Jesus when he broke the bread.

Even as they spoke Jesus himself appeared in the room. Many of them were afraid, for they thought that he was a spirit. But when he showed them the wounds in his hands and feet they knew who he was.

Jesus was to appear to his disciples many times before he left them to ascend into heaven and go to his Father, God. Forty days were to pass before his Ascension, and these days are often called 'The Great Forty Days'.

Your turn now . . .

Research and writing

Write in your own words details of each of the following.
a) The happenings on the road to Emmaus.
b) The happenings in Cleopas's house.
c) The happenings in the Upper Room.

Finding out

1 Write down the answers to each of the following questions.
  a) How far was it from Jerusalem to Emmaus?
  b) What was said to Jesus when the three travellers arrived in Emmaus?
  c) What did Jesus say when he greeted the disciples in the Upper Room?
You will find the answers to these questions by reading Luke, Chapter 24, verses 13, 29 and 36–40.

2 Draw what Jesus ate in the Upper Room. To do this you will need to read Luke, Chapter 24, verse 42.

—— 32 ——

The Great Forty Days

In Chapter 31 we read how Jesus appeared to two disciples on the road to Emmaus and later to the disciples in the Upper Room. Thomas had not been with the others, and when he came in they told him:

'We have seen the Lord.'

Thomas would not believe what they said.

'Unless I see the marks of the nails in his hands I will not believe,' he told them.

About a week later the disciples were in the Upper Room again. This time Thomas was with them. Suddenly Jesus appeared in the room. He spoke to Thomas.

'Look at my hands,' he said, 'and believe.'

Thomas knew that it was Jesus.

A few days after this Peter said to the others,

'I am going fishing.' The others went with him. All night they fished but they caught nothing. In the morning they saw a man on the shore. It was Jesus, but they did not know him.

'Have you any fish?' he asked.

When they replied that they had caught nothing he told them to let down their net on the right side of the boat. The disciples did so and at once their net was filled with fish, so many that they could not pull it into the boat.

'It is the Lord,' said John.

When Peter heard this he jumped into the sea to swim to the

The disciples let down their net on the right side of the boat.

shore. The others came in the boat, pulling the net after them. When they reached the shore they found a fire lit, fish and bread. They sat down to eat. Not one of them asked the man who he was, for they knew now that it was Jesus.

Once more Jesus appeared to his disciples. This time it was at Bethany. Here, as he lifted up his arms to bless them, he was taken from them and ascended into heaven. The disciples went back to Jerusalem full of joy, and went out to carry on the work of Jesus, preaching to the people and healing the sick.

Your turn now...

Research and writing

Write one paragraph on each of the following.
a) Thomas;
b) the fishing trip;
c) why the disciples went back to Jerusalem.

Drama

With some friends act out the story of the fishing trip. Think about what simple props you might use to make your drama more effective. It might be best to perform it in three short acts.

Note

Write down the following in your book:
Palm Sunday – Jesus' entry into Jerusalem
Good Friday – the day of Jesus' crucifixion
Easter Day – the day on which he rose from the dead – the Resurrection
Ascension Day – the day on which he ascended into Heaven
Can you find out the actual dates on which these days fall this year?

—— 33 ——

Jesus teaches how to Pray

Jesus often went away alone to pray to his Father, God. One day his disciples asked him to teach them how to pray. He taught them the words the we know so well as 'The Lord's Prayer'. He also told them two stories to show that God is always ready to hear our prayers.

One night, when a man and his family had gone to bed, there was a loud knock at his door.

'Lend me some bread,' said a voice, 'for a friend of mine has just come to see me and I have no food to give him.'

At first the man would not get up from his bed, but his friend outside kept on asking. At last he got up and gave him what he wanted, so that he would not worry him any more.

'So you must keep on asking when you pray,' said Jesus, 'and God will give you what you ask for.'

One night there was a loud knock at the door.

The other story is about a judge who was not a very good man. He did not care about God or anybody else, but only about himself. A widow woman in his town kept coming to him to ask for help. For a long time he did nothing to help her. But at last, so that she would not bother him any more, he did what she wanted.

'This judge,' said Jesus, 'who was not a good man, helped the widow woman because she kept on asking him. If you keep asking God, who is good to all people, then he will help you too.'

Another story that Jesus told about prayer is about a Pharisee and a publican. (In Chapters 9 and 10 we read that the Pharisees were leaders of the Jewish religion, and the publicans were tax-collectors.) These two men went up to the Temple to pray, and this is what the Pharisee said:

'O God, I do thank you that I am a good man, and not like other men who are evil, or even like that tax-collector. I fast twice every week, and I give away a tenth of all my money.'

The tax-collector stood on one side and all that he could say was, 'God have mercy on me, for I am a sinner.'

'God will hear the prayer of this second man,' said Jesus, 'for he is humble. But he will not hear the prayer of the Pharisee who is proud of his goodness.'

Your turn now...

Research and discussion

With your friends and teacher discuss each of the following in as much detail as possible.
a) The story of the man who knocked at the door.
b) The story of the Pharisee and the publican.

Writing

Answer each of the following questions with a sentence.
a) What did the disciples ask Jesus to teach them to do?
b) What quality needed for prayer is shown in the story of the man knocking on the door?
c) How would you describe the judge?
d) How would you describe the Pharisee?
e) How would you describe the publican?

Illustration

Choose one of the stories and illustrate it. Underneath your picture write some words from the Bible which are about it. The passages in the Bible are: Luke, Chapter 11, verses 9 and 10; Chapter 18, verses 1, 13 and 14.

The Unforgiving Servant

In Chapter 33 we read what Jesus taught his disciples about prayer. Remember the words that we say in 'The Lord's Prayer':

The servant took hold of him and told him that he must pay.

'Forgive us our trespasses as we forgive those who trespass against us.'

Jesus told his disciples that they must not ask God to forgive them if they were not ready to forgive those who did wrong to them. Peter asked Jesus, 'How often must I forgive anyone who does wrong to me? Must I forgive him seven times?'

'No!' said Jesus, 'not seven times. You must forgive him seventy times seven.' By this Jesus meant that we must keep on forgiving all the time. Then he told the disciples a story to show them what he meant.

There was once a king whose servants owed him money. One servant came to him who owed him a very great sum of money.

As he was not able to pay, the king said that he must be sold as a slave, with his wife and children and all that he had, so that the debt could be paid. The servant fell at the king's feet and asked for more time so that he could pay his debt. The king was very sorry for him and forgave him all that he owed.

When the servant went out he found another servant who owed him just a small sum of money. He took hold of him and told him that he must pay. This servant fell down at his feet and asked for time so that he could pay. But the first servant would not listen to him and had him put into prison until he paid all that he owed.

The other servants were sorry when they saw this and went to tell the king. The king was very angry and sent for the first servant.

'You wicked servant!' he said. 'I forgave you all that great debt when you asked me. Why did you not have pity on the other servant and forgive him what he owed you?'

Then the king put him in prison until he was able to pay all the money that he owed him.

'That is what God will do to you,' said Jesus, 'if you do not forgive other people.'

Your turn now . . .

Research and discussion

Read Matthew, Chapter 18, verses 23–35. This is a PARABLE, which means a story with a lesson to teach.

What is the lesson in this story? How is it made clear?

Writing

1 Write down the meaning of the following words. Use a dictionary where necessary:
trespass   debt   forgiven   owed.

2 Imagine you are the servant who reported what the ungrateful man had done.

Try to write down the exact words you would say to the king. Remember you are indignant, angry and want to see 'fair play'.

Drama

Act out any scene from this parable.

The Prodigal Son

In the story of the Unforgiving Servant in Chapter 34, we read what Jesus had to say about forgiveness. One of his most wonderful stories is about a forgiving father. It is called the parable of the Prodigal Son. The word 'prodigal' means wasteful, and we shall see how wasteful he was.

A rich man had two sons. The younger one asked him for his share of his father's money, and the father divided his money between the two sons. It was not long after this that the young son went off to another land. Here he wasted all his money having a good time. He had many friends to help him to spend his money, but when it was all gone he found no one to help him.

At this time there was a great famine in the land and the young man was hungry. He had to find some kind of work. At

The prodigal son comes home.

last he got a job looking after pigs. He was so hungry that he could even have eaten the pig food. As he sat there, dirty, hungry, his clothes in rags, he began to think about home. Why, even the servants had clean clothes and plenty to eat. He would go home and ask his father to give him work as a servant: he was no longer worthy of being his son.

So the son set off for home. When he was still a long way off his father saw him and ran out to meet him. He was full of joy that his son had come back at last.

'I have done wrong,' said the son to his father. 'I am not worthy to be your son. Make me your servant!'

But his father did not listen to him. He told the servants to bring out new clothes, shoes and a ring, and then to kill the fatted calf for them to eat. The fatted calf was kept for a special time and this time had now come.

When the elder son came back from his work in the fields he heard music and dancing and asked a servant what it meant. As soon as he heard about his brother he was angry and would not go in. His father came out to bring him in.

'Father,' said the elder son, 'I have always worked hard for you. I have always done what you told me. Yet you never gave me even a kid to share with my friends. But now my brother has come home after wasting all your money and you have killed the fatted calf for him!'

'All that I have is yours, my son,' said the father. 'But it was right for us to be glad, for your brother who was lost is found again.'

Your turn now...

Research and writing

Read Luke, Chapter 15, verses 11–32. When you have done this answer the following questions.
a) What did the younger son say to himself as he looked after the pigs?
b) What did the father do when he saw his son coming home?
c) What did the father say about his son?

Drama

With one or two of your friends choose a part of this story which

you would like to act out.
    Pay particular attention to what the characters actually say to each other in your drama.

Illustration

Draw three pictures of the Prodigal son:
a) when he was enjoying himself away from home;
b) on his journey home;
c) as he is reunited with his father.
Think about his facial expressions and his clothes when you draw the pictures.

—— 36 ——

The Good Shepherd

When Jesus told stories he often talked about the people who lived in Palestine. These were stories about builders, tax-collectors, Pharisees, farmers, fishermen and women. There

The sheepfold.

were many sheep in the land and sometimes Jesus spoke about the sheep and their shepherds.

Once Jesus said, 'I am the door of the sheep.' He was talking about the sheepfolds that were to be found in the hills. They were made of stones with thorns on top of the walls. (See picture, p.82.) Here the shepherds could bring their sheep and keep them safe at night from robbers and wild animals.

In Palestine shepherds did not drive their sheep in front of them: they led the way and the sheep followed because they knew their shepherd. They knew that he would lead them to grass and water. To keep near the shepherd was to keep safe.

Jesus also called himself 'The Good Shepherd'. If only the people would follow him they would be safe, as the sheep were safe when they followed their shepherd. A good shepherd was always ready to fight any enemy and would even give his life for his sheep.

'Once there was a man with a hundred sheep,' said Jesus. 'He lost one of them, so he left the ninety-nine and went out in the dark to find the one that was lost. When he found it he was full of happiness and asked his friends to come and join with him in his joy over the lost sheep that had been found. There is joy like this in Heaven,' Jesus went on, 'when a sinful man becomes good.'

As he looked around Jesus must have seen some women in the crowd and he told a story for them too.

'There was a woman who had ten silver coins,' he said. 'One of these coins was lost in the house.' It may have fallen into a crack in the mud floor. 'So the woman lit her lamp, for the inside of the house was dark. She took her brush and began to sweep. At last she found her lost coin and asked her friends to come in and join her in her joy at finding the coin that had been lost. There is joy like this in Heaven,' said Jesus, 'when a sinner becomes good.'

Your turn now . . .

Research and writing

Write at least one sentence about each of the following.
a) The sort of people Jesus talked about in his stories.
b) Sheepfolds.
c) How Palestinian shepherds controlled their sheep.
d) The story of the coins.

Drama

You now know the stories of the missing sheep and the missing coin. Make up a drama of your own which makes the same point as these two parables.

Notes

In St John's Gospel there are many statements by Jesus in which he says: 'I am the . . .'. Finish this sentence in each of the different ways shown in Chapters 6, verse 35; 8 verse 12; 10 verses 7 and 11; 11 verse 25; 14 verse 6; 15 verse 1.

—— 37 ——

The Rich Man and Lazarus

One day Jesus was in the Temple, in the Court of the Women. (See the diagram of the Temple in Chapter 22.) Here there were thirteen offertory boxes into which the people put their gifts for the Temple. Jesus saw the rich people giving big sums of money. Then a poor widow came along and put in a penny. Jesus turned and spoke to his disciples.

'This poor widow,' he said 'has put in more than all the others. They have given out of their wealth, but she has given all that she had.'

Another day a rich young man came up to Jesus and asked him what he must do to get to heaven.

'Keep the commandments,' said Jesus. 'Do not kill, steal, lie or cheat, and honour your parents.'

'I have kept these commandments all my life,' said the man.

'There is one other thing,' said Jesus. 'Go and sell all that you have and give to the poor. Then come, and follow me.'

The young man went away sadly, for he was very rich. Jesus turned to his disciples and told them how hard it was for those who loved riches to get into heaven. He told them a story about a rich man.

There was once a very rich man who had a fine house, clothes and food. At his gate sat a beggar named Lazarus, dirty and covered with sores. He longed for a few crumbs from the rich man's meals. At last the two men died. The beggar went to heaven and the rich man to hell. The rich man cried out to

Lazarus sat at the rich man's gate.

Abraham, whom he could see with Lazarus in heaven:

'Father Abraham, send Lazarus to cool my tongue with water in these flames.'

But Abraham told him that while he was alive he had all the good things while Lazarus was poor and ill. Now Lazarus was happy and he had to suffer in the flames.

'Then let Lazarus go and warn my brothers so that they will not have to join me here,' said the rich man.

'No!' said Abraham. 'They must learn from the words of the prophets, the men of God, and then they can escape your punishment.'

In this story Jesus showed that you must do good with your riches before it is too late.

Your turn now . . .

Research and writing

Answer each of the following questions with a sentence.
a) What were the offertory boxes?
b) Why wouldn't the rich young man go with Jesus?
c) What did the rich man do for Lazarus whilst they were alive?
d) What happened to the rich man and Lazarus after their deaths?
e) What lesson did the rich man learn after he had died?

Illustration

Draw the scene in the Temple where the poor woman is putting her penny into the offertory box.

How might she be feeling? How might the rich people be looking at her? Who is paying the greatest attention to her? Try to show these things in your drawing.

Note

Write down the following information in your book.

DIVES – means 'rich man'. The story is sometimes called 'Dives and Lazarus'.

ABRAHAM'S BOSOM – the name given to the place where good Jews went after death.

— 38 —

Wisdom and Folly

In Chapter 37 we read what Jesus said about riches. He told one story about a man who was rich and foolish.

This man had a very good farm. He had so many crops that he had no room to store all his grain. So he made up his mind to pull down all his barns and to build bigger ones. Then he could fill them and sit back in comfort.

'I can take my ease,' he said, 'and eat, drink and be merry.'

But God told him that he was foolish, for that very night he was to die. Then what good would all his riches be to him?

'That is what happens to the man who thinks only of his riches and not about God,' said Jesus.

Jesus had been teaching his disciples and the people in what we call 'The Sermon on the Mount'. At the end of his sermon he said:

'The man who hears my teaching and tries to do what I say is like a wise man who built his house on a rock. When the rain and the floods and the wind came they did no damage to the

The wise man built his house on the rock. The foolish man built his on the sand.

house, for it stood on a rock. But the man who hears my words and does not do what I say is like a foolish man. He built his house on sand. When the rain and the floods and the wind came the house fell, for it had no firm foundation.'

Jesus told another story about wise and foolish people. This one was about ten girls who were waiting for the bridegroom at a wedding. Five of them were wise and five were foolish. All of them had taken their oil lamps and those who were wise had taken jars of oil to fill up their lamps. The foolish ones had taken no extra oil. While they waited they lay down to sleep. About midnight there was a shout:

'The bridegroom is coming: go out to meet him.'

At once the ten girls began to get ready. The lamps of the five foolish ones had gone out and they tried to borrow some oil from those who were wise.

'No!' said the wise girls, 'there may not be enough for you and for us as well. Go to the village and buy some.'

While the foolish girls were away trying to buy some oil, the bridegroom came to the house. All those who were ready went in with him to the wedding. Later the five foolish girls came back. But the door was shut and they could not get in.

The lesson of this story is found in two well-known words: 'Be prepared.'

Your turn now . . .

Research and discussion

With your friends and teacher discuss the following.
a) Why was the rich farmer foolish?
b) Why is a well-built house like a good person?
c) What is the lesson of the story about the girls at the wedding?
d) The Sermon on the Mount – Matthew, Chapters 5–7.

Drama

With a group of friends act out the story of the girls at the wedding. The following words may give you ideas:
cautious – 'it'll be alright' – excitement – panic – prepared – welcomed – appreciated.

Illustration

Draw a dramatic picture of the house collapsing in the storm. Add a caption to say why it collapsed.

Note
Print 'BE PREPARED' in your book and put a suitable pattern round it. .

39

The Three Servants

In Chapter 38 we read how Jesus told people that they must 'Be prepared'. This is the motto of the Boy Scouts and the Girl Guides. Jesus also told people some words that every Wolf Cub will know: 'Do your best.' God gives everybody a chance to work for him: some do better than others. Some try: others do not. The story that Jesus told was about three servants.

The third man hid his money in a hole in the ground.

'A rich man had to go away to another land. Before he went he called three of his servants and left them to look after his money. To the first he gave a thousand pounds, to the second he gave four hundred pounds, and to the third, two hundred pounds. Then he went away.

'The first servant used his master's money well and very soon his thousand pounds had become two thousand. The second man, too, did very well, and his four hundred pounds became eight hundred. But the third man hid his two hundred pounds in a hole in the ground.

'After a long time the master came back home. He called his three servants to him to ask what they had done with his money. How glad he was to hear that the first servant had made another thousand pounds for him.

' "Well done!" he said. "You have been a good servant. I shall give you more important work to do for me."

'When the second servant came to him the master was glad to hear that he, too, had doubled his money.

' "Well done!" he said. "You have been a good servant. I shall give you more important work to do."

'Then the third man came in and his master asked him what he had done.

' "I was afraid," said the man, "and hid your money in the ground, so that it would be safe when you came back. See, here it is."

'The master was very angry.

' "Why didn't you put my money in the bank?" he asked. "Then at least I should have had some interest."

'The third servant was sent out in disgrace.'

Your turn now . . .

Research and writing

1 Write one paragraph on each of the following.
   a) The servant who received one thousand pounds.
   b) The servant who received four hundred pounds.
   c) The servant who received two hundred pounds.

2 In your own words write two letters.
   a) One should be from the rich man to a friend. It should describe his feelings about what happened with his servants.
   b) The second should be from you to a newspaper's 'good advice' column. In it you tell this whole story in your own words. End it by saying: 'You must always do the best with what you have got.'

Drama

Act out three short scenes of each servant receiving his money. In each scene act out: the servant discussing what he should do with the money; taking action; his master's response.
   Try and show the personality of each servant in your dramas.

40

The Sower

One day Jesus was by the Sea of Galilee. The crowd was so big that he went and sat in a boat a few feet from the shore. From the boat he spoke to the crowd and told them this story.

'A sower went out to sow his seeds. As he went along he took the seeds from the basket in front of him and threw them out, first to one side then to the other. Some of the seeds fell on the path that ran across the field. Very soon the birds came down to eat them up. Some seeds fell where the ground was rocky and there was little soil. They began to grow, but when the hot sun came out they died, for there was no water in the soil. Other seeds fell at the side of the field, where there were weeds and thorns. These, too, began to grow, but they were soon killed by the weeds.

'The rest of the seeds fell on good soil. They grew up tall and strong, with a good ear of corn on each stem. Some of these ears of corn had thirty seeds in them, some had sixty, and some had a

A sower went out to sow his seeds.

hundred.'

The disciples had often seen the sower at work so this story was easy for them to follow. But they did not know what lesson Jesus was trying to teach them. They asked Jesus to tell them what the story meant. This is what he told them.

'The seed is the word of God and the soil is like the people who hear it. Some people are like the path: they hear God's word but do nothing about it. Some people are like the rocky, shallow soil: they hear God's word and believe it for a time, but very soon they forget all about it. The soil full of weeds and thorns is like the people who hear God's word and for a while try to do what is right. But after a time the word of God is choked by other things like money and worry.

'The good ground is like the people who hear the word of God and then do what God tells them. Just as the corn grows and ripens, so they live good lives and help others to do the same.'

Your turn now...

Research and writing

1 Answer each of the following questions with a sentence.
  a) How did the sower spread the seed?
  b) What happened to the seed which fell on the path?
  c) What did the seed which fell on the rocky ground lack?
  d) What killed some of the seed?
  e) Did the ears of corn all have the same number of seeds?

2 In your own words write a short account showing what this story means.

Illustration

Draw a picture showing the sower throwing the seed.

—— 41 ——

The Good Samaritan

A Lawyer once came to Jesus and asked him a question.
'What must I do to get to heaven?' he asked.

The Samaritan went up to him and tended his wounds.

'What does the law say?' asked Jesus.

'You must love God and you must love your neighbour,' the lawyer said.

'That is right,' said Jesus. 'That is what you must do if you want to get to heaven.'

'But who is my neighbour?' asked the lawyer. And Jesus told him this story.

A man was going along the road from Jerusalem to Jericho when he was set upon by robbers. They took his clothes and all that he had and left him half dead.

Soon a priest came along the road. He may have been going up to Jerusalem to help in the worship at the Temple there. When he came to the place where the man lay he looked at him and went past on the other side of the road.

Then a Levite came by. The Levites were men who helped the priests. They also helped in the Temple worship by singing and getting the sacrifices ready. The Levite came over to look at the man who lay at the side of the road and then he, too, went past.

At last another man came by. He was a Samaritan. The Samaritans were not Jews and the Jews and the Samaritans hated one another. They never spoke unless they had to. But this Samaritan did not think about the fact that the man who lay there was a Jew. He went up to him and tended his wounds with wine and oil: the wine was to wash his wounds and the oil was to heal them. Then he put him on his ass and took him to an inn. There he looked after him until he had to go on his way. He gave the innkeeper some money to take care of the wounded man and told him that if it cost any more he would pay him back when he came again.

After he had told this story Jesus turned to the lawyer.

'Which of the three men was the neighbour of the man who was attacked by the robbers?' he asked.

'Why, the one who helped him,' said the lawyer.

'Then you go and do the same,' said Jesus.

Your turn now . . .

Research and writing

Answer each of the following questions with a sentence.
a) Who asked Jesus' advice?
b) What was the route of the traveller's journey?
c) What did the robbers steal from the traveller?
d) What is a Levite?
e) Who was the least helpful person of all?
f) Was the Samaritan concerned that the injured man might be a Jew?
g) Did the Samaritan worry about having his money repaid?

Drama

Act out this story in detail. Try to capture the real atmosphere. Think about the following words: journey – worried – attacked – no chance – unconscious – frightened – hurried – looked but took no action – gave help regardless – complete the job of helping.

Illustration

Draw a scene from the story.

The Story of a Vineyard

In the last week of his life Jesus was often in the Temple. It was here that he told the people a parable about a vineyard.

A man who owned some land made a vineyard. He put a hedge round it and in the middle he built a watch-tower. Then he made a press where the grapes could be crushed for wine. When all was ready he put some men in charge of his vineyard and went off to another land. These men are called 'husbandmen' in the Bible: it is a word that means farmers.

When the grapes were ripe the man sent some of his servants for the money from the crop. But the husbandmen were wicked men and they wanted the money for themselves. They beat one of the servants, threw stones at another and killed a third. The owner sent more servants but the husbandmen did the same thing to these.

At last he sent his own son, for he was sure that they would not dare to harm him. But when he came to the vineyard the husbandmen said:

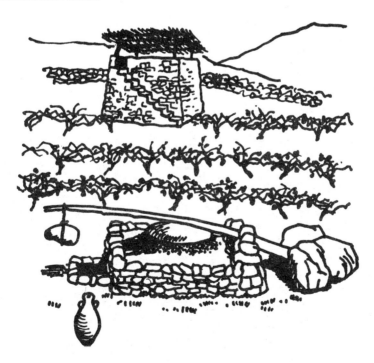

The watch-tower and the wine-press in the vineyard.

'Here comes the owner's son. Let us kill him and then the vineyard will be ours.' So they took him and killed him.

'What will the owner do?' asked Jesus. 'He will come and kill these wicked men and find good men to look after his vineyard.'

When the priests and Pharisees heard this they were very angry. They knew that when Jesus told this story he was talking about them. He was, for this is the meaning of the story.

The vineyard is the land of Palestine and its owner is God. The vines are God's people and the husbandmen are the priests and Pharisees who are there to care for the people. The servants are the prophets of the Old Testament. These were men chosen by God to tell his people about him and how they ought to live. The prophets had often been ill-treated and even killed in the past. The son in the story is Jesus himself and he tells how the priests and the Pharisees are going to kill him.

It was no wonder that these men were angry with Jesus, but they did not dare to touch him then because they were afraid of the people.

Your turn now . . .

Research and writing

1 Read this story again very carefully. Then make a list of what all things and people in the parable really stand for. The first two are done for you:

Owner – God

Vineyard – Palestine.

2 a) Study the picture of the wine press and then say how you think it works.

b) What did the husbandmen sell to make money?

3 Write out in your own words what the priests and Pharisees did when they heard this story. Read Mark, Chapter 12, verse 12 to find this information.

Drama

Act out one of the scenes from this parable. Try to make your characters speak in exactly the way the story suggests. The following words might give you ideas: hope – try – forgive – certain – cruel – selfish – greedy – ruthless.